First published in Great Britain by
Simon & Schuster UK Ltd 2008
A CBS Company

ISBN 9 78184 737 1560

Simon and Schuster UK Ltd
Africa House
64–78 Kingsway
London WC2B 6AH

1 3 5 7 9 10 8 6 4 2

Design and illustrations by Jane Norman
Text by Sheila Purcell
Jacket design by Lizzie Gardiner
Printed and bound in China

Contents

Introduction

Congratulations, you're a granny! The new
arrival is miraculously beautiful, highly
intelligent and all-round adorable (not that
you're biased, of course). The moment you set
eyes on him or her, you make a silent vow to be
the best grandmother ever. It's a promise that's
easy to keep, for having grandchildren
in your life is a delight.

As a granny you have unlimited devotion and
decades of experience to draw on. Your trusting
grandchild has boundless curiosity and an
unfettered imagination. These practical tips for
spending happy time together will strengthen
that special bond.

"I feel I've been put on earth to love my grandchildren."

Dr Miriam Stoppard, b. 1937

Get Cooking

Be prepared

Baking never fails to satisfy. Clear worktops
of clutter and put dampened tea towels under
plates and mixing bowls to stop them slipping
about. Remember to put sharp knives
well out of reach.

First steps

Encourage toddlers to grate cheese, rub slivers
of butter and flour into a crumble mix, mash
potatoes and beat eggs for an
omelette or cake.

✳

Cut oranges in half so that they can squeeze
the juice to drink or make into ice lollies.

Simple starters

Flour and water is the ideal combination for
busy toddlers. Help them make scones,
biscuits and jam tarts and let them peep
through the oven door to see the raw
ingredients turn brown in a short
space of time.

＊

Put margarine on a double thickness of kitchen
paper so that they can grease a cake tin.

＊

Teach older children how to bake fairy cakes,
gingerbread men, bread and butter pudding and
flapjacks. They can also scrub and prick
potatoes for baking and prepare the fillings.

Fairy cakes

Cream 100 g (3½ oz) butter and 100 g (3½ oz) caster sugar together until pale and light textured. Beat in two standard eggs, one at a time. With each one, add a tablespoon of flour from 100 g (3½ oz) sifted self-raising flour. Fold in the remaining flour with a metal spoon. Spoon the mixture into 18 paper cases in a bun tin. Bake the cakes for 20–25 minutes at Gas Mark 5/190°C/375°F until well risen and golden. Cool on a wire rack.

❋

For variations, stir 50 g (2 oz) currants, sultanas or plain chocolate chips into the mixture after beating in the eggs. Add decorations, kept in place by a dab of icing. Give children an icing pen to draw a pattern or their name or initials on top – a tradition that children still love.

"Pat-a-cake, pat-a-cake, baker's man,

bake me a cake as fast as you can;

Pat it and prick it and mark it with 'B'.

And put in the oven for baby and me."

Nursery rhyme

Butterfly cakes

Slice off the top of each fairy cake and put a
heaped teaspoon of whipped cream over the
cut surface. Cut the top in half and arrange like
butterfly wings on top of the cream.
Dust with icing sugar.

Cooking by numbers

Talk to them about ingredients and count the
pieces as they put them into the pot or bowl.
Encourage children to smell and taste things.

Hands-on bread

Yeast-free soda bread is fun to make. Preheat the oven to Gas Mark 6/200°C/400°F. Put 170 g (6 oz) plain flour and the same quantity of self-raising wholemeal flour in a large mixing bowl. Add half a teaspoon of salt and half a teaspoon of bicarbonate of soda and stir. Make a well in the centre and pour in 290 ml (½ pint) buttermilk. Mix quickly with a fork to form a soft dough, adding a little milk if the dough is too stiff. Shape into a round and cut a deep cross on the top. Place on a lightly floured backing sheet and bake for about 30 minutes or until the loaf sounds hollow when tapped. Cool on a wire rack.

"The Queen of Hearts she made some tarts,
all on a summer's day."

Nursery rhyme

Fast food

Let older children thread cubes of cheese,
chopped cooked chicken, chunks of celery,
carrot or cucumber and cherry tomatoes on to
a wooden skewer, leaving enough room to hold
at both ends. Serve with warm pitta bread.

Repeat the process for pudding, using cubes of
fresh and dried fruit and grapes.

Fun with fruit and veg

Prepare ready-made bases and a range of toppings for children to make their own DIY pizzas. Put out colourful ingredients to make a pretend face – olives, slices of pepper, cherry tomatoes, strips of carrot and small pieces of broccoli.

Set out small portions of fresh and dried fruit, which children can add to pancakes, ice cream or jellies.

Offer a selection of fresh fruit to make into smoothies and milk shakes.

" *An apple a day keeps the doctor away.* **"**

Anon.

Fruit fool

A traditional fool mixes cream with fresh or cooked fruit. This healthier variation uses plain yoghurt. Gently wash 450 g (1 lb) of raspberries, reserving 115 g (4 oz) for decoration. Put the remainder in a bowl and sprinkle with 30 g (1 oz) sugar. Leave for a few minutes, then blend fruit and sugar in a liquidiser. Stir the purée into 150 ml (5 fl oz) of Greek yoghurt. Top with the remaining berries.

Baked apple

Core one large cooking apple per person and cut a line around it two-thirds from the top, just enough to break the skin. Stuff the core space with 15 g (½ oz) of raisins and one teaspoon of honey. Put the apples in a dish with enough water to cover the bottom. Bake at Gas Mark 4/ 180°C/350°F for 45 minutes or until the apples are tender. Serve with custard or ice-cream.

Honey baked bananas

Take four ripe bananas and place each one in a square of foil. Sprinkle with a little soft brown sugar and squeeze of lemon juice, then drizzle with a teaspoon of honey. Fold to make a foil parcel and bake in a hot oven for 10 minutes.

Picky eaters

Involve children in planning and preparing their meals.

＊

Serve small portions – they can always have 'seconds' if they like it.

＊

A banana or some strawberries liquidised with milk and served in a sundae glass with a corkscrew straw is nutritious and may tempt children who refuse food.

＊

Cut sandwiches into novelty shapes with biscuit cutters.

Arrange food into pictures – a mashed potato
hedgehog with small sausages for spikes
and broccoli for trees.

Encourage children to talk about food in fairy
tales and nursery rhymes, such as Goldilocks,
The Gingerbread Man and The Queen of Tarts.
Perhaps make some simple jam tarts
or gingerbread.

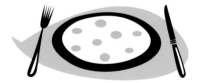

" *They dined on mince and slices of quince,*
Which they ate with a runcible spoon. **"**

Edward Lear, 1812–1888

Time to dine

Let children call the rest of the house to a meal
with a bell or gong. Ask them to sit at the head
of the table or turn meal times into a special
occasion by announcing a high tea or tea party.
Invite them to have a late supper,
on a tray, with Granny.

> **❝** *Red sky at night, shepherd's delight; red sky in the morning, shepherd's warning.* **❞**

Author unknown

The Great Outdoors

Pooh sticks

Winnie the Pooh invented this game of dropping sticks on one side of a bridge and waiting to see which one would appear first on the other side.

Weather forecast

Look at the sky together and teach children familiar weather sayings *'Enough blue in the sky to make a pair of sailor's trousers.'* *'Rain before seven, fine before eleven.'*

✳

" *It's raining, it's pouring;*
The old man is snoring. **"**

Nursery rhyme

Out and about

Children are always thirsty, so take a bottle
of water when you go out.

✳

Take your camera – children love to see
pictures of themselves. Encourage older
children's visual awareness by letting them
take snaps of things that interest them.

Flowers and seeds

Show them how to make daisy chains
(a darning needle could be a useful accessory
if your eyesight is not what it was).

✹

Save seeds in an envelope with a label – your
grandchild can sow their own seeds next year.

✹

Collect tree buds to look up and label, flowers
and leaves to dry, acorns, conkers
and pine cones.

Flower press

Put flowers between sheets of blotting or kitchen paper and press inside a heavy book for several days.

Energy to burn

A simple obstacle course is a great way for older children to let off steam in the garden. Use tables and chairs to climb over and under and a paddling pool or washing-up bowls to wade through. Prop up a piece of wood against a wall or tree to run up and jump off. Chalk a route around the side of the house or garage.

✳

Teach older children how to wash a car. Kit them out with a plastic apron or anorak, wellies, a bucket of warm soapy water, cloths and an old chair to stand on to reach the roof.

Water cricket

Play with a plastic bat and balloons
filled with water.

Races

Three-legged, egg and spoon and sack races
always appeal.

" What I love best are the little things... the drawings fixed on the kitchen wall, the songs, and the story readings. **"**

Dorothy White, WI granny

Art and Crafts

Finger puppets

Stick felt eyes on to the fingers of old rubber or knitted gloves to make puppets.

Plan ahead

Have a special place for storing materials such as old tissue boxes, kitchen roll holders, thin pieces of card, scraps of foil, fabric and wool, left-over wrapping paper, ribbons, coloured tissue, egg boxes, cotton reels, yoghurt pots, old greetings and Christmas cards.

Stock up on child-safe glue, poster paints, brushes, fat crayons, string and glitter.

This is me

Buy a roll of cheap lining paper. Lay a metre length or more on the floor and ask your grandchild to lie on it with arms and legs slightly outstretched. Trace their outline with a thick crayon. He or she can use paint, crayons and scraps to create hair, eyes and clothes for a life-sized self-portrait.

❝Grandparents are similar to a piece of string – handy to have around and easily wrapped around the fingers of their grandchildren.❞

Anon.

Playdough

Home-made playdough is much cheaper than the ready-packaged version and can be baked in a moderate oven until hard, ready to be painted.

✳

Mix together one cup of plain flour, half a cup of salt and two tablespoons of cream of tartar. Add one cup of water and mix until smooth. Add the food colouring and then two tablespoons of oil. Cook on a medium heat and stir regularly until the mixture forms a smooth ball. Leave to cool. Store in cling film or in a container in the fridge. Once it starts to crumble, mix up a fresh batch.

✳

Repeat the process using different food colourings.

*" Anyone who has never made a mistake
has never tried anything new. "*

Albert Einstein, 1879–1955

Paint magic

Cut potatoes in half and cut simple patterns.
Coat the raised pattern with poster paint and
press down on paper to make prints.

✺

Add a dollop of glue to paint, brush on to paper
and use an old comb to make patterns.

✺

Using two colours, paint thickly on one half of
the paper. Press firmly to the plain half while
still wet for a mirror image.

✺

Paint toddlers' palms and press them firmly on
to paper for hand prints.

✺

Use clothes pegs to hang up wet paper to dry.

" *Every child is an artist. The problem is how to remain an artist once he grows up.* **"**

Pablo Picasso, 1881–1973

Pasta jewellery

Macaroni makes quick and easy jewellery.
Paint, then thread on to a string to make
a necklace or bracelet.

Egg shell art

Wash and crush egg shells to paint and use for
mosaic patterns.

Boxing clever

Extra-large containers for fridges and other appliances can quickly be transformed into a house, castle or spaceship. Cut out doors and windows to suit and draw on extras such as wheels or curtains.

Turn a TV or computer box into a robot: cut holes for the arms and eyes and add foil decorations. Smaller boxes will double up as cars or a train with carriages, connected with string.

A shoe box makes a cosy bed for toys. Or, line it with felt, coloured paper or pretty material then let children paint the outside and glue it with shells, odd sequins and fabric scraps to make a box for treasures.

*"Mary, Mary, quite contrary,
how does your garden grow?
With silver bells and cockle shells,
And pretty maids all in a row."*

Nursery rhyme

Green Fingers

M is for Mary

Rake and smooth a patch of soil, then mark out
the first initial of your grandchild's name with a
stick. Let them sow the furrow with seeds or
seedlings and keep it watered.

"And then – she found herself at last in the beautiful garden, among the bright flower-beds and the cool fountains."

Lewis Carroll, 1832–1898

"March winds, April showers, bring forth May flowers."

Anon.

A patch of garden

Give children their own small patch of garden.
Help them plant it with daffodil, tulip, grape
hyacinth and crocus bulbs for a bright
spring show of colour.

Herbs are resilient and grow quickly. Plant
rosemary, thyme, mint, sage and parsley in
your grandchild's garden plot or in pots or
window boxes. Children can add herbs to
soups, salads and home-made
summer drinks.

How does your garden grow?

Give tots a small plastic indoor watering can to
help you sprinkle the garden. Use waste water
where possible and consider installing a
water butt with a tap.

Blooming marvels

Colourful, fast-growing annuals such as sunflowers and candytuft give quick results and are a great way to cultivate an early interest in gardening. Large seeds such as marigolds, sweet peas and nasturtiums are easier to handle. Sow in pots or straight into the child's plot.

✳

If space allows, plant a butterfly bush – buddleia – along with lavender and catmint to attract bees.

Shower surprise

On a hot day when children are in swimsuits,
ask them to pretend they're a flower and
sprinkle them with a watering can.

❋

*"My garden is my most beautiful
masterpiece."*

Claude Monet, 1840–1926

Growing veg

Even if you have only a tiny outside space,
children can plant tomatoes in a bag, potatoes
in a bucket and lettuce in plant pots.

※

Email or send pictures of their growing flowers
and veggies. Try to arrange a return visit
when their crops are ready to pick.

" *The juicy green apple known as Granny Smith is named after the woman who first cultivated it, Maria Ann Smith of New South Wales, Australia.* **"**

A is for apple

If you have an apple tree, cut out the child's initial in black paper and stick it on a fruit in early summer – remove the paper in the autumn when the apple has ripened.

"The rain is raining all around
It falls on field and tree,
It rains on the umbrellas here,
And on the ships at sea."

Robert Louis Stevenson, 1850–1894

Rainy Days

Indoor picnic

Put a blanket over the table with a tablecloth underneath and turn lunch into an indoor picnic.

Keeping little ones happy

Small children will spend happy hours playing with water at the kitchen sink – protect the floor with old towels.

✳

Toddlers and babies who can sit up will enjoy being creative with a set of upturned saucepans and a wooden spoon.

✳

Play hand-clapping and counting games:

'A sailor went to sea, sea, sea, to see what he could see, see, see. But all that he could see, see, see, was the bottom of the deep blue sea, sea, sea.'

Sing and dance

Teach older children tongue twisters and old music-hall songs such as *Daisy, Daisy.*

✳

Teach them the twist and how to jive or do the conga through the house.

✳

❝ *Come dance a jig*
To my Granny's pig. **❞**

Nursery rhyme

❝ There were ten green bottles, hanging on the wall, ten green bottles, hanging on the wall and if one green bottle should accidently fall, there'd be nine green bottles hanging on the wall ❞

Traditional counting song

Picture this

Look through family photo albums and tell them about the funny or naughty things their parents did as children – and anecdotes about eccentric relatives.

✳

Draw a basic family tree on a large sheet of thick paper or board. You could photocopy old and new snapshots, cut them out, and stick a 'portrait' next to each entry.

❝ *...never formerly had the grandmother been so beautiful and so tall. She took the little maiden on her arm and both flew in brightness and in joy.* **❞**

Hans Christian Andersen, 1805–1875

Tidying

Children love to feel useful. Over fives can sort
a button box into different sizes and colours
and help you tidy up cupboards.

Old favourites

Unearth their parents' old toys and books if
you've kept them and tell the grandchildren
which were their favourites.

Let's pretend

Keep a dressing-up box with old hats, scarves, bags, sunglasses, cheap costume jewellery, Grandad's old waistcoat – anything that three-year-olds and upwards can use to play different people. Look out for similar items in charity shops.

✳

Hold a tea party for dolls or teddies with toy-sized portions of real or playdough food on plastic plates. If you have a doll's tea set, your grandchild might like to lay the table or pour pretend tea.

For a shop: put tins and packets on one side of a cardboard box, with a shoe box as a till and a supply of one and two pence coins. Save old receipts or cut up small pieces of paper.

An old white shirt with rolled-up sleeves and upside-down watch drawn on will kit out young doctors, nurses and vets to treat poorly toys. Give them a bag with plasters, a bandage and a plastic spoon to administer pretend medicine.

Games

Play simple card and board games – Happy
Families, Snap, Snakes and Ladders.

✳

In the garden, 'Grandmother's footsteps' is fun
for older children, from three upwards.
Granny sits 20 or 30 feet away with her back
turned. The child or children creep towards her
without making a noise. Each time she turns
around, they must stop and stand still. If
Granny sees anyone's feet moving, she sends
them back to the start. Whoever gets to her
first, becomes the 'granny'.

"I've had a text from Granny – she's going to throw a party for you.**"**

Prince Harry, b. 1984
(to Mike Tindall, England rugby player).

"She was quite simply the most magical grandmother you could possibly have."

Prince Charles, b. 1948

Coming to Stay

Hidden treasure

If the parting from parents is tearful, distract
children with a treasure hunt. The treasure
could be a clue to the fun still to come –
crayons, a mini gardening set, a packet
of seeds or toy stationery.

Preparing for their visit

Have a special cupboard or drawer reserved
for their things.

✳

Stock up on a second-hand highchair, cot and
pushchair. Check charity shops and car boot
sales for toys, games, doll's tea sets, Lego, and
books. Ladybird and Puffin titles offer a wealth
of bright ideas for things to do, along with
classic fairy tales, stories and nursery rhymes.

✳

Free up time by preparing and freezing food
ahead of their visit.

Coming to Stay

❝ *There's no place like home,*
except grandma's. **❞**

Anon.

67

My life so far

Compile a memory scrapbook of their life so far with date and place of birth, weight, first photos, pictures of their home, mementos of family outings or holidays. Update it together on each visit.

✵

Take a picture of your grandchild in the same place each time they stay, to mark how quickly they are growing and add it to the memory book with the date.

✵

Record their growth each year by marking their height on a wall or cupboard door with a pencil and ruler.

"No cowboy was ever faster on the draw than a grandparent pulling a baby picture out of a wallet."

Anon.

Time together

French knitting – do a little each day and stitch a mat to take home as a present.

✳

Prick large holes around images on old greetings cards and show children how to sew, using a darning needle and wool.

✳

Keep a weather chart during their visit.

✳

Near Christmas, let them unpack tree decorations or put them away on Twelfth Night.

✳

Read a chapter of their current favourite book each night before bedtime to help them wind down. Let early risers join you in bed to read a story or comic.

" *And so our mothers and grandmothers have, more often than not anonymously, handed on the creative spark, the seed of flower they themselves never hoped to see...* **"**

Alice Walker, b. 1944

Outings and expeditions

Children love an expedition with Granny – just the top deck of a bus is fun. Hop on an open-air bus to see the sights.

✷

Take time to watch the hustle and bustle of city life. Younger children love watching builders and bulldozers, delivery vans and window cleaners on ladders.

✷

Enrol children of all ages at your local library, if they don't already have a card. You can spend a happy hour or two looking at and choosing books. Libraries often have special events for children, a storyteller or someone who reads to them.

Useful websites

The National Trust organises seasonal activities for children at its properties throughout the year. Check details on the Trust website – if you don't have a computer, you can access one at your local library. **Goodgranny.com** and **mumsnet.com** are other useful websites with lots of ideas and tips for outings and activities.

❋

Look at the RoSPA website for an update on safety issues.

Quiet time

Grannies need quiet time too. Rent or buy
some children's DVDs in advance to keep them
entertained for an hour so – ask their parents
what they'd prefer them to watch.

"Reading is to the mind what exercise is to the body."

Sir Richard Steele, 1672–1729

**" Perfect love sometimes does not come
until grandchildren are born. "**

Welsh proverb

**" Grandmas hold our tiny hands for just a
little while, but our hearts forever. "**

Author unknown

Long-distance Granny

Your treasures may be hundreds, even thousands of miles away but you can still build up a warm and close relationship with the help of modern technology. Emails, digital photos phone calls and faxes all bring a sense of immediacy – but remember that children also adore receiving post.

At regular intervals, send a padded envelope (a separate one for each child) with a long newsy letter, photographs, copies of old snapshots and a small present. It doesn't cost much and will remind your grandchild that he or she is always in your thoughts.

"March and April...sprinkled the lanes with golden-eyed celandines, whose bright enamelled petals glittered like glass..."

Alison Uttley, 1884–1976

Marking the Seasons

A seasonal album

With your grandchild or children, make a special
photo album of your garden or surrounding
countryside at different times of year. Stick the
photos in the album and let them decorate a
page for each season with a
drawing or pattern.

Spring is coming

Celebrate the longer days with pancakes and decorated Easter eggs.

Blowing eggs for painting

Before blowing an egg, wash it. Dry the egg and stick a piece of sellotape on the pointed end (to stop the egg shell from cracking). With a pin, make a hole at the pointed end for blowing through and a larger one at the other end for the liquid egg to escape. Gently blow the egg out of its shell into a cup.

❋

" *Don't teach your Granny to suck eggs.* **"**

Old saying

Coloured eggs for Easter

Put hard-boiled eggs in a glass bowl of hot water with a tablespoon of vinegar, then add food colouring. The acid in the vinegar helps the dye to stick to the eggs.

✳

Colour eggs with natural ingredients. For yellow, mix three teaspoons of turmeric with water and vinegar. For red, use cranberry or cherry juice or add a small slice of beetroot to very hot water. For green, boil eggs in spinach water.

✳

To make patterns, stick narrow strips of masking tape before colouring the eggs. Remove the tape when the eggs are dry.

" Summer is icumen in
Lhude sing cuccu."

Traditional English round

Lemonade for a summer picnic

Pack a picnic and take homemade lemonade.
Squeeze the juice of four lemons and pour into
a pint jug. Add four tablespoons of caster sugar
and enough boiling water to dissolve it. Top up
with cold water and leave in the fridge.

Sunshine games

Put a buttercup under your grandchild's chin to
see if he or she 'likes butter'.

✳

Blow dandelion clocks to practise
counting the time.

Holiday schemes

Check local sports centres and swimming pools. Many have sessions for over-threes and special pools or areas for toddlers.

Seashells by the seashore

On a trip to the seaside, collect shells, stones, sea grass and scraps of seaweed to use for scrapbooks and shell boxes.

❝ *Flopsy, Mopsy and Cottontail, who were good little bunnies, went down the lane to gather blackberries.* **❞**

Beatrix Potter, 1866–1943

Autumn activities

Go blackberry picking, then make a
crumble with apples.

✳

Scrunch through leaves and collect interesting
coloured ones to glue on to a painting of a tree
trunk to make your own picture of a tree.

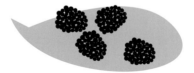

Hedgehog hideaway

Create a safe home for hibernating hedgehogs.
Take a large, thick cardboard box and cut out
two side air vents of 15 cm x 5 cm and an
entrance of 15 cm in diameter, facing south if
possible. Put shredded newspaper inside with
dry, clean grass or straw on top. Cover the top
of the box with a small piece of plastic sheeting,
such as a carrier bag, cut open. Place twigs
around the box to create a dome shape and
cover with dried grass and leaves. Position the
hideaway near a hedge in a sheltered place.

Bulbs for Christmas

Put hyacinth bulbs in special glasses filled with
water and a little charcoal to keep it fresh.
Do not wet the bulb.

" Laura arrived on this scene on a cold December morning when snow lay in deep drifts over the fields and blocked the roads. "

Flora Thompson, 1876–1947

Christmas cards and tags

Save old Christmas cards to recycle as gift tags. Use pinking shears or scissors to cut out pictures, making sure there is no writing on the reverse. Make a hole in one corner with a hole-puncher and use coloured string or ribbon to attach the label.

Simple Christmas presents

Use poppy heads, leaves and dried grasses to
decorate a calendar or cut a piece of felt as a
bookmark and decorate it with cut-out
pictures or dried flowers.

Food and drink

Put out food and water for the birds. If you have a bird box, nail it to a tree. Give your grandchild a pair of binoculars for watching the birds.

✳

Pack hot food picnics with soup, sausages and drinking chocolate on crisp, frosty days.

" *Starlight, star bright,*
The first star I see tonight,
I wish I may, I wish I might,
Have the wish I wish tonight. **"**

Nursery rhyme

Star bright

On clear nights, go outside to see the moon
and stars. Stick 'glow in the dark' stars
on the ceiling in the children's bedroom.